THE
ANGEL
STORIES

TRUE STORIES OF SOME OF THE ANGELS
IN OUR LIFE, HOME AND MINISTRY

MICHAEL VAN VLYMEN

ISBN-13: 978-1975686611
ISBN-10: 1975686616

DEDICATION

To all of you who love to hear stories of God's faithfulness and divine protection. May God give you many, many angel stories of your own to encourage and inspire others.

CONTENTS

NTRODUCTION

This book contains some of the amazing and inspiring interactions and visitations from angels our family has enjoyed for the last several years. We have learned through these encounters that God is ever-present and indeed has given His angels charge over us. I hope that these stories bless you and inspire you and cause you to know that His angels are always around you.

One thing I want to share is that I share these encounters with respect, but as normal interaction with Heaven. I don't want anyone to think that this is something so over the top and unusual that it won't happen to them. Angels appeared to people all throughout the Bible. As believers in Christ, we can expect that they will also appear to us.

**Please note..... This book is a compilation of accounts of visitations of angels that we have had, that have also appeared in other books that present teachings etc. I have been asked by many people for two years now to make a book available with <u>only</u> positive and uplifting angel stories. So...Thanks!

1

Angels Watching Over Us

One evening in 2011, my daughter Angie and I were leaving the house to go work out together at the gym and My son Matt had left with friends. My wife was busy cleaning the house. (I know. I should have probably stayed home to help her.) Not too long after we had all left, my wife Gordana was vacuuming the stairs in the front entryway.

She was lost in her work when suddenly a man walked past her in the entryway of our home.. As he passed, she saw him from behind as he walked around the corner toward the living room.

Gordana said at first, she had thought it was me. The man was dressed in clothes like the ones I had been wearing. She said that from behind he looked very similar to me, but was in better shape. That may have been what tipped her off. She then realized that I had already left the house to go to the gym. Gordana followed the man into the living room but discovered he had disappeared.

For a minute, Gordana said that she was fearful but also thought that it might have been an angel, so she prayed,

"Lord I thought angels are supposed to have wings." Gordana said that the Lord immediately spoke to her. "No, some angels appear as men." Then she was at peace.

Be not forgetful to entertain strangers: for thereby some have entertained angels unawares. (Hebrews 13:2 KJV)

When we came home Gordana shared with us the excitement of her evening. This was an amazing event in our household. I believe it was either the first, or one of the very first encounters that my wife Gordana had ever had with an angel. It increased the faith of us all to believe for more!

2

Guardian Angels

One morning I woke up very early, perhaps three or four a.m., and I decided to lay there in bed and pray and ask the Lord to show me or teach me something. I laid very still and let my eyes slowly move about the room looking with a real expectation that the Lord would do it. When I looked toward the north west corner of our bedroom, I saw something that overwhelmed my senses a bit. There was a warrior angel standing in the corner. He was facing away from me so at first I only saw his back. He was standing motionless, facing west. When I gathered my senses enough to realize what I was seeing with eyes wide open, I was completely awestruck. I said "Wow!" in response. As soon as I had said "Wow!" he turned and looked right at me with the most serious of expressions on his face. I only got to see him for perhaps fifteen or twenty seconds altogether and he was gone from view. I thought about it for a long while and was finally able to return to sleep. I thought , how awesome it is that the Lord protects us so faithfully!

3

Meeting Sam

I had just finished a three day fast, where I spent time praying, worshipping and waiting on the Lord several hours a day. I don't recall anything extreme happening during the actual fast and I didn't record anything real significant in my journal during that period. On the night at the end of my fast, I went to sleep and was enjoying a nice peaceful sleep when all of the sudden I heard someone (A man) whispering my name. "Mike...Mike!" Knowing that there was no reason for a strange man to be in our bedroom, I got an adrenaline rush, sprang out of bcd and attacked the intruder.

I fought for everything I was worth and all I could think of was to do everything I could do to protect my family and try not to get hurt. As I "fought" with the intruder, there came a point within only several seconds that I realized that something was very wrong. I suddenly realized that my "opponent" was extremely big and very powerful and I was having no effect on him. I also realized that he was "play fighting" with me much like someone might do with a child.

It was then that I realized that I had attacked an angel. This angel, I realized was pretending to fight me and all the while laughing at me so hard it's a wonder he didn't hurt himself! When I think back on the occasion I really have a nice laugh myself.

After I calmed down and he stopped laughing, this angel introduced himself to me as Sam. He told me a little bit about his ministry and also relayed the fact that he was assigned to our family during a time when my parents went to a Bible college for missionaries, in Waukesha, Wisconsin when I was about ten. Sam told me that he desired to have more people assigned to him, but he said that is a choice that we make. We have to decide whether to go on in the Lord or not and thus that determines the angels who are assigned to us.

Sam is quite large, probably eight and a half feet tall and very muscular. He has dark bronze skin and short dark hair. He kind of looks like a more handsome version of the Rock, Dwayne Johnson. And as you already know from this story that he has a great sense of humor, but he also has a really nice smile and a very engaging personality.

When Sam showed up he had brought me a basket filled with bread. Being overwhelmed at the time, I forgot to ask him the significance of this gift. But I asked the Lord later and He told me it was food for my spirit and soul. It was strength and nourishment, it was revelation, it was the word.

4

Contending With Angels

As strange as the previous experience was with the angel called Sam, you might think that this type of encounter with angels is not a common one. We sometimes think of encounters with angels being some dramatic and powerful word delivered from God or a moment of supernatural protection. Indeed they are that and more. What I have discovered in my own life and that of my family is that angels, like people, have personalities and can have a more intimate relationship with us if we allow it. Just like in the Bible where they broke bread with Abraham, we can have that as well.

1 And the Lord appeared unto him in the plains of Mamre: and he sat in the tent door in the heat of the day;
2 And he lift up his eyes and looked, and, lo, three men stood by him: and when he saw them, he ran to meet them from the tent door, and bowed himself toward the ground,
3 And said, My Lord, if now I have found favour in thy sight, pass not away, I pray thee, from thy servant:
4 Let a little water, I pray you, be fetched, and wash your feet, and rest yourselves under the tree:
5 And I will fetch a morsel of bread, and comfort ye your hearts; after that ye shall pass on: for therefore are ye come to your servant. And they said, So do, as thou hast said.

(Genesis 18:1-5 KJV)

My wife Gordana and I were ministering in a small church in the Virgin Islands last year and we were staying in the home of the Assistant Pastor and his wife. The atmosphere in the home was one of prayer and seeking God.

During the very early hours of the morning, I could not sleep so I thought maybe I would pray as I lay there in bed. As I was pondering this, suddenly I felt someone jump on me and pin my arms by my side, to the bed. At first I was completely startled, as you do not normally expect things like this to happen, but when I opened my eyes, I saw another angel with a huge smile on his face trying to get me to wrestle with him.

This angel was black and wearing off-white clothing. He was probably six feet tall as best I can judge and had very intense but kind eyes that were a green – hazel color. You could almost feel the laughter and joy coming from him.

I struggled against him a bit, but of course to no avail. I finally said *"What are you doing?! I'm trying to sleep!"* When I said this, still laughing he jumped off of me and flew away.

I thought to myself *"My goodness! What could be next?!"*

Then, after pondering these encounters for a while, a strange thought entered my mind. What if these angels all talk to each other and laugh about some of these things? I could just picture that angel saying to his friends, "You should see this crazy guy Mike. He thinks he can wrestle with us! It's really funny! Go check him out!"

So I have been wondering... who's next?

5

A Trip Behind the Scenes

For a long time I had thought that the Lord was going to give me a Land Rover as a ministry vehicle. I came to this conclusion because almost every time that I would be in serious prayer while out driving around, I would see a Land Rover. I would be praying up a storm and look to my right or left and lo and behold, there beside me would be a Land Rover of some sort.

I was very excited that an angel came one night and told me that he was taking me somewhere for my ministry vehicle! In the spirit, this angel took me to a big building that looked like an airport terminal building. I came to understand by the Spirit, that this was an angelic logistics center. As we came up to the building, I saw an extended passenger van next to the building and the angel told me that this was my ministry vehicle. When I questioned him in my mind, he explained that the Land Rover was not practical for the work the Lord had for me to do and the extended van would hold many more people for God's purposes. I then understood and agreed completely.

Then the angel motioned me to go with him into the building

and to the top. When we got to the top, we were actually on the top of the building. As I looked around, I saw that there was a very fast paced amount of angelic activity going on. Angels with documents and papers and angels coming and going. It was a very serious and business like environment. As the angel and I stood there by the entrance door, the angel said "Wait here." I watched him as he walked over to a very large desk in the center of the "room" and leaned over to the angel seated at the desk and spoke something very close to his ear.

The angel at the desk, cocked his head to one side and kind of looked at me over his shoulder. It was a very, very serious look.... I remember thinking that this angel looked like a very intense Gary Busey. (The actor) Very rugged, handsome and all business. He then responded to the angel who had brought me there, and went back to his other business on the desk.

After the angel with me had spoken to the other angel, his demeanor changed quite a bit. Previously he had been more serious and business like and now he had a big smile on his face as he approached me. He was genuinely excited! I could see it on his face.

He got up close to me and told me that the angel in charge had also given me a very significant gift for my ministry, and he told me what that gift was. I was stunned. I was stunned by the gift and stunned by the fact that he said it was for my ministry. I didn't even know I had one! I wish I could share a little more about the gift but I am not as yet releases to do that.

6

The Angels in the Office

The same angel who took me to the logistics center has come to take me to several other places as well. That seems to be part of his ministry. When I have a need for something, he has been one to address the need and give me help or get help for me.

This angel also took me to an office once. He appears and says "come with me" and the next thing I know I find myself going somewhere with him. This time we entered into a small office with the top half of the walls being windows. It resembled some old fashioned newspaper movie office and was very warm and inviting. In the office he introduced me to two other angels. The two angels apparently had something to do with office type work and were also going to be helping me in "my ministry". I have seen some very serious members of the angelic host in the past, but it seems like the angels most closely associated with my life and family and work, the day to day stuff, have a real affection for us and a joy in what God is doing in our lives!

The two angels I met in the office were as excited as the one who took me there to meet them. They both shook my hand

and said how excited they were to be a part of what God was doing in my life. I told them it was going to be great working together with them. You can't help but be encouraged when even the angels are excited for what God is doing with you!

7

Overwhelming Angelic Response

Many times before we go to bed at night, we blow the shofar as a way to set the spiritual atmosphere in the house. It seemed to bring a peace and presence of the Lord that we could feel in the house. It had been perhaps a month or so after we had purchased the shofar and brought it into our home, when the following occurred.

We had blown the shofar several times in our bedroom and then we went to bed. My wife Gordana sometimes (many times) is praying in intercession for others about bedtime and this day was no exception. I decided that I would go downstairs to pray. I went to the living room and sat down in my "prayer chair" (a large comfortable chair I like to sit in while I pray) I prayed for an hour perhaps and then at some point I fell asleep. When I woke up, I woke up in the spirit realm. That is, when I awoke my spiritual eyes were wide open. I looked around me and saw perhaps fifty angels all around me standing in groups and talking to each other.

I was in awe. I was drawn to two very big angels who were standing just to my right, talking to each other. They looked like very powerful warriors approximately eight feet tall and they were dressed in similar attire. The clothing they wore was what you might expect a warrior to wear when not in battle. They wore heavy tunics, light in color with their arms uncovered. One of the angels had blond hair and one had dark hair, both about shoulder length.

I don't know what they thought about me, because when I saw them, I went over to them and just kind of stood there gawking at them. (In my own defense, they presented a pretty awesome appearance) They continued their conversation, unaffected by my presence and I was able to hear some of the things they were talking about. I recognized the angel with the dark hair as one who had spoken to me once before about a year or so earlier. He was easy to remember because he had reminded me of Mel Gibson from the movie "Braveheart."

This encounter really made me think about what it means to blow the shofar and what Heaven releases when we do.

8

The Men From El Salvador

The great thing about having angels around to help us is that they are always prepared. You will never hear them tell you "Sorry, we'd love to help you but we didn't bring the right tool for the job." Angels also don't charge you for their help. They are working for your Father on your behalf.

It was mid-January in Indianapolis and it was cold. The streets were covered in a deep snow that the snow plows had not gotten cleared away yet. The streets were slushy and messy, and ruts had been carved into the streets by the vehicles traveling over them. At work, I was dispatched to an old industrial type neighborhood to a company to do some repairs. I did the work and after I left and drove a few blocks, I realized the my left rear tire was flat. I didn't relish the idea of changing it in this weather but I have changed tires in bad weather before.

I soon discovered that the truck I had been given to drive that day had no jack. It had a spare tire, but no jack. Great! I was aggravated but not completely thrown by it. I didn't know immediately what to do so I just stood there next to the truck thinking and looking around.

There was no one out and about. It was too cold. All the houses in the area were run down and appeared very uninviting to me. I was hesitant to knock on any doors.

Some movement suddenly caught my eye and I looked up. I saw two Hispanic looking men walking down an alley towards me. When they got to me, they motioned towards the truck as if to say "what's up?" I told them that I had a tire but no jack. They didn't talk much at all. I thought that perhaps they didn't speak English that well, so I began to speak to them in Spanish. They were still not speaking to me. I kind of got the idea then that they could talk, but just chose not to. One of the men told me "wait." Then they disappeared back down the alley.

Not two minutes later I see them once again coming toward me, but this time they were pulling a big floor jack behind them. They all but ignored me as they changed the tire and they would not even allow me to help them. One of the men told me that he didn't want me to get my hands wet and cold. After a few minutes they were finished and I took out a twenty dollar bill to pay them. They were not interested in the money and would not accept it.

Just before they left me, I asked them where they were from. They both told me twice *"We are from El Salvador."* Then they walked away back down the alley.

It was only later as I replayed the day's events in my mind that I realized what had happened. Two men just happened to show up exactly when I needed help. They just happened to have exactly what was needed to help me and then even though I was a stranger to them, they were still concerned about my being cold and wouldn't allow me to help. And to top it off, would not accept money.

And where, of all the places in the world had they come from? El Salvador.....The Savior. They had said "We are from the Savior."

9

Harold the Angel

The Lord tests our hearts. If you haven't thought too much about the possibility of entertaining angels unaware, you probably should.

Be not forgetful to entertain strangers: for thereby some have entertained angels unawares. (Hebrews 13:2)

One of the churches that we attend is situated in a neighborhood that is impoverished. There are many times when people show up in the church basement after church for only the fellowship hour because there is food always provided. Just like in any church, there are some that welcome the strangers and give them food and encouragement, (One of the women in the church who regularly sees angels is always loving to these people. There may be a lesson there.) and there are some that don't.

One day after the fellowship time, I had lagged behind to talk to friends and when I finally made it out of the church, there was a group of five or six people in the church parking lot gathered around an older gentleman who looked like someone who might be down on his luck. (So to speak) I walked over to the group, not saying a word to my wife who happened to be there, and tried to give the "homeless" man five dollars.

He looked me in the eye and said "That's not necessary. Your wife has already given me money." That slipped past me at the time. The fact that he knew one of those women was my wife and that it indeed was the same one that had given him money should have told me something.

Something else that struck me as odd was that a person who is having a hard time making it does not turn down money. What the man said to me next kind of turned the lights on for me. He told me that his name was Harold. I asked him if he had been to any of the other churches in the area? (meaning to ask for help) The way he answered me was delivered in a very matter of fact way that said "I am on assignment." He said "I visit all the churches in this area" as he looked me in the eye a little longer than was comfortable. Then he thanked us and left. I believe that Harold was an angel.

10

Rebuked by an Angel

Who in the world would admit to being rebuked by an angel? Let me just say it's a good thing. It lets you know that God is ever present to keep us on the right path.

On this day, I had gone grocery shopping with my wife and mother in law. As we were walking across the parking lot towards the entrance of the grocery store , a woman on a cell phone pulled into the parking lot seemingly narrowly missing an elderly woman walking. When the woman on the cell phone got out of her car, she was still in conversation oblivious to what had just happened.

I tried to dismiss it and move on, but couldn't seem to do it. I mulled it over and over in my mind, "How rude and reckless of her", "She needs to know about this" etc.. After about ten minutes of entertaining these thoughts, I went and found the woman in the store. She was still involved in conversation as she shopped and I approached her.

As I approached her, I noticed a rather large man standing to my left with an empty shopping cart. He was just standing there looking at me. For some reason I said to myself, "I think he is a priest." I walked past the man and approached the woman. I began telling her about what she had done, how she had almost run over the old woman and that she needed to be more careful and aware. The woman began to disagree and argue with me and she told me that it never happened, which made me even angrier.

As I continued to talk to the woman, the "man" pushed his cart in between the woman and I and looked at me. He said "You need to walk away." I ignored him basically and continued to argue with the woman. He again said "You need to walk away." I still continued to argue with the woman. The third time he told me to walk away, I took a step toward him to talk to him and I felt something that made me shake violently. I took a step back from him and the shaking stopped. The realization then swept over me that even though this man was quite large and had pushed his cart between us, the woman had never even looked at him. Even though he had spoken several times, telling me to walk away, the woman never acknowledged him at all.

Everything came together for me in an instant. I knew then that he was an angel and that I had better do what he is telling me to do. I felt repentant. I was sorry I had spoken to the woman in such a manner. I apologized over and over. I kept muttering "I'm so sorry, I'm so sorry."

As the woman walked away and the man began to walk away, I thought to myself ,"That is not like me at all. Why did I do that." The man suddenly turned and answered my thought. He said " She didn't answer you the way you thought she should." Then he walked behind the magazine rack and I turned my head for an instant and he was gone. I went around the corner to see if maybe he was still there, but he was gone. I felt the fear of the Lord upon me as I realized that I had ignored his instruction three times. I realized that I need to be more aware and more loving.

11

The Angel Over the Mall

My wife Gordana used to work at a salon in a shopping mall about twenty minutes from our house. One day I borrowed her car to use for the day. I figured that I would just pick her up at the end of her day. The only variable in this was, if my wife had more clients or customers show up after I got to the mall, I would either have to wait for her to finish the extra work, or leave and make a return trip.

Wouldn't you know that *this* day was one of *those* days. I had actually gotten to the mall about a half an hour early, and then I found out that my wife had just committed herself to two more hours of work. I was looking at a two and a half hour wait. I didn't really want to drive home and waste the driving time or the gas, yet I didn't really want to hang out in the mall for two and a half hours. You can only cruise the food court for free samples so many times before they start looking at you funny. What was I to do?

I suddenly got a brilliant idea! Why don't I do a prayer walk around the mall! That would kill a lot of time and I would actually be doing something useful, changing the spiritual atmosphere. So I set out on my prayer walk. I walked around the interior of the mall, praying out loud in tongues. Sometimes I walked into the various stores and sometimes I did not. I sang in tongues a lot as I went because it's a way of praying that makes you look like less of a nut. People sing right? Well after one lap I still had loads of time, so I did another lap. After the second lap, I still had way too much time left, so I decided to move my prayer walk to the outside of the building. I then began walking around the outside of the mall. I didn't realize until I began, that going around the outside of the mall would be considerably more walking! But I had committed myself. I did my prayer walk around the mall and made it back to the main entrance, a little tired but spiritually refreshed.

I still had about twenty minutes of free time so I headed to the food court. I figured I could use the facilities and get something to drink. I came out of the restroom and walked out into the food court portion of the mall.

As I walked into the food court, a handsome young black man in his mid-thirties approached me. He smiled and held out his hand and shook mine and said "I want you to know that I appreciate your being here today." I was a little confused at that point. There was something in the way he spoke that carried something more than just his words. Then he spoke again, but this time he spoke to my mind and all confusion was immediately cleared up.

He said "I am the angel over this mall." and he turned and walked away.

I have since done many more prayer walks at the mall, but have not seen him again.

12

The Voice of an Angel

Many times the Lord has to make us aware that we don't know it all. I had seen so far at this point in my life probably several hundred angels. I had not gotten blasé about seeing angels at all, but perhaps I was not giving them the respect that they are due. They are after all, beloved and powerful servants of the Lord.

One late night as I sat in my prayer chair waiting on God, I suddenly became aware of a powerful angelic presence that entered the room and was in front of me just to my left. I waited to see what would happen. I was not aware just how powerful this angel was until he began to speak.

As this angel spoke, the sound of his voice carried so much power that I could not handle it. The sound of his voice vibrated through me as the words hit me. The sound of his voice shook me to the core and all I could receive was... "My name is ..... and the message is..." I literally ran from my chair and out of the room. From listening to others who encounter angels and other heavenly beings, I have heard that sometimes the visitations are hard to handle.
I heard Neville Johnson of The Academy of Light speak

about the power of sound in the spirit realm. He said that the rank or authority or power of an angel can be carried by their voice. I got to experience this first hand.

That's one thing about encountering God's angels, there is never a time when it becomes "ordinary". It is always special.

13

The Angel Returns

On the second of May, I was again in my prayer chair seeking the Lord when I fell into a dream. In my dream, I was sitting in my prayer chair praying and waiting on God.

As I waited on the Lord, I began to hear a radio broadcast that was talking about a message for the children of God, the servants of the Lord. I was actually at times a little aggravated that someone was interrupting my prayer time by playing this broadcast. I remember thinking "who is playing the TV in the middle of the night? Everyone knows this is my prayer time." I was not able to receive and understand all of the message, but at the end of the "broadcast" I realized that I recognized the voice and had heard it before. It was the voice of the same angel I had been overwhelmed by, except this time his voice was carried to me in a dream, and I could handle it!

I have since asked the Lord many times that He allow this angel to return and give me the opportunity to be exposed to his powerful voice again, but as yet, it has not happened. We can be sure God's timing is best.

14

Angels Will Check You Out

One Saturday morning I woke up at about 3:30 am and went to my prayer chair to pray. That night, I worshipped for a while on my knees to acknowledge Jesus' lordship over my life, and then I prayed in tongues for an hour or so. Sometime between 5 and 5:30 am, I must have fallen asleep. I then woke up in the spirit, that is to say, with my spiritual eyes open, to see "someone" looking at me with his face only inches away from mine.

It took me a minute to understand what was going on, and as I began to have awareness that an angel was looking into my face, he slowly backed up a little, continuing to watch me and then he stood up fully. This angel looked very much like me, but he had longer hair. He was about six feet tall, trim and wearing white clothing of some sort. Once I was fully aware of what was happening, he disappeared from view.

I have since learned that when someone is trying to exercise their spiritual senses, the angels are very excited for us and will help us in any way that they can. They have been close to my face many times, and it is as though they are looking at us and wondering "are you awake yet?"

15

The Angel with Bleeding Eyes

Early one morning I was praying and waiting on the Lord. As I sat there in my prayer chair, my spiritual eyes opened and I could see an angel in the distance. He looked fairly young, maybe thirty or so, and was dressed in off-white clothing and his hair was blonde and shoulder length. I could tell that he was on his way somewhere. At first, I was hesitant to engage him because I didn't want to leave being in the spirit by calling out to him. . But I decided to ask him to help me anyway..

I called out to him "Hey! Can you help me?" The angel turned from his previous path and came toward me. When he was close, he asked me "What can I do for you?" I could not immediately hear him, but I read his lips. I answered him "I want my eyes to see and my ears to hear." Then his eyes suddenly took on the look of having been injured and they were bleeding. For some reason, I thought he was trying to trick me. I said "What are you doing? I know you're an angel of the Lord." At that time, his eyes became normal again and that's when he told me, "Your eyes and ears have been damaged by all the garbage you have put into them. But the Lord Jesus can heal them." And having said that, he then turned and walked away.

If you are someone who is pursuing spiritual sight, or seeing in the spiritual realm or fellowship with angels and Heaven, be careful what you expose your eyes to. If you have a past of looking at things unclean, repent and ask the Lord to cleanse and heal your eyes.

16

Angels Minister to Us

If you like the idea of angels working I and around your life, I would encourage you to ask the Father to send His angels to minister to you. Please don't be afraid of getting out of balance. As long as your heart and your focus is the Lord Jesus, you can be sure that you are on safe ground. The Lord knows your heart and your desire for Him.

He will lead you and keep you from deception. The point is that angels do know how to minister. They are very effective ministering spirits and just as you shouldn't hesitate letting a godly person pray over you, don't hesitate accepting angelic ministry either.

One night I woke up thinking about the angelic servants of the Lord and I asked the Lord to send an angel to minister to me. I had no idea at the time what that might look like, but I knew that I wanted it. After I prayed I was looking around the room expecting the Lord to answer my prayer. I was waiting and looking. Suddenly I saw an angel approaching me. He had walked through the wall and into our room, then taking a few more steps over to the bed where I lay. He was dressed like you would expect a knight to be dressed and moved in a very purposeful way towards me . The last thing I remember about this encounter was him kneeling on one knee at my bedside and stretching out his hand over me. At that point I was knocked out. I don't know exactly what happened after that, but knowing the Lord and how great He is, I know it must have been good!

"...You have not because you ask not." (James 4:1)

Are not all angels ministering spirits sent to serve those who will inherit salvation? (Hebrews 1:14 NIV)

17

Angels and the Spirit Realm

It was a Friday morning and I was looking forward to something exciting coming. I didn't know what that excitement might be, but I know it's coming because I start the day in prayer. Really? Starting the day in prayer is exciting? Well, not for religious people it probably isn't but for Kingdom people it can be an adventure! Much of the revelation and visitation I have had from Heaven as well as other experiences of an otherworldly kind have been born out of prayer. I know that anything could happen, and for me that is exciting!

Somewhere in the midst of my prayer time, I found myself standing in a strange place. It was a place in the spirit realm, that I associate with regions or places of captivity of the soul. (If you don't know what that is, Ana Mendez has written a book on this subject and explains it very well.) But in a nutshell, it is a place where people are "captive" by the enemy for one reason or another and that captivity drastically influences their everyday lives in the natural realm..

As I stood there at the entrance of this vast spiritual place, I saw many people who had various problems . Some people had sicknesses and others traumas or other bondages holding them. Among the group, I saw someone in there that I knew. I could see what it was that was afflicting him and I knew this to be true. I myself have been captive in such places and there is nothing like freedom from them. I decided I was going to go in and rescue him. I felt a holy anger rise up in me and I started to enter this place.

As I came into the entrance, an angel stood there before me. I looked at him questioning what his appearance was all about. He said "You can't go in there." Now I have spoken to a few angels and some have given me instruction or rebuke as the situations called for, so you think I would know enough by now to listen when they speak. I looked at him and said "Really? I can't go in there? Watch me." I know that sounds really bad but I was not trying to be difficult. I was passionately moved to try to help someone and my passion overcame my good sense.

The angel did not rebuke me or prevent me from going in. He immediately turned to another angel and said "Go with him." It was not apparent to me why this other angel was sent in with me, but as I found myself getting stuck in dead-ends in this strange place, he was always there to open a door for me to go through or make a way for me to get out. I encountered many unusual things in this place and in the end, I was brought out and shown by one of the angels that the man I was concerned about would be delivered by the Lord. The Lord had it all under control. Thank you Jesus!

God is faithful like that. The angels knew that I was not needed in that place, but God in His mercy allows us to navigate through situations like this so that we can grow up. We need to grow up into spiritual things and not be ignorant about the unseen realm. To many, this will sound like a fantasy. Many have no idea that a spirit realm even exists. But aren't you glad that as we grow and learn His angels protect us? I know I am.

18

Lord, Teach Me to Pray

Towards the beginning of my journey into the deeper things of God, I sincerely tried to make that deeper connection with the Lord, but with little understanding of how to do it. I would go on long prayer walks and pray for hours, seeking direction from the Lord and also His blessing, anointing and gifts etc.. My prayers were very sincere but quite wrong. I was planning out everything in my mind that I wanted God to do as if I had to instruct Him what to do and how to do it. To make this clear, here is an example.

"Lord please cleanse me (so I can receive your infilling) and sanctify me (so I can be set aside for your purposes) and baptize me (so I can move in your power) then Lord provide me with ministry funds and provision (so I can have the means to go where I am called to go) and then open opportunities (so I can bring salvation and pray for the sick, etc.) In Jesus' name, amen."

I had it all laid out for Him.

I also prayed in the best King James English I could muster up gleaned from years of exposure to people I had heard that prayed very beautiful and poetic prayers that way. (not necessarily anointed though unfortunately)

On the surface this prayer really doesn't look all that bad. That's the stuff we are supposed to be doing right? The problem here was that I was not allowing the flow of Holy Spirit in my prayer or life. I had everything planned out already of what I wanted God to do and how He should do it. What if He wanted to anoint me first and then do something else second? That's His business and all I have to be is a willing and obedient vessel. (which I now know)

After a long time of faithfully praying like this, I began to get very weary and frustrated. What more could I do? I was making myself available to God and He was not responding! I was fed up and I spent three days telling Him so!

For three days in a row I went on my prayer walk solely to talk to the Lord about my frustrations and my apparent incompetence in prayer and seeking Him. This was my new "prayer model" during that three day period...

"Lord I do not have a clue. You know I want to be like those men whose testimonies I love so much, but I don't know what to do. I know that you are probably talking to me but I can't hear you. I've spent most of my life unaware that you even still speak and I can't hear you now. Please shake me and get my attention and tell me what to do."

I prayed this prayer over and over on my prayer walks. I also would like to interject that this prayer does not qualify as vain repetition because I meant it every time I prayed it!

Of Course You Can See!

On the night of the third day something quite spectacular happened. I had done my prayer walk that day and then came home and got ready for bed. I lay down and went to sleep.

Have you ever had an experience where someone tries to wake you from sleep by laying their hand on you and gently shaking you? Well, that is not what happened to me!

As I lay sound asleep, suddenly I felt someone stick their hand into my chest and shake me violently, thus waking me up. At this point I was absolutely terrified and the thought going through my mind was "Jesus please let this be You!" I was immediately then fully awake, and was aware that someone was grabbing me by my feet and then pulled me off the foot of the bed, and onto my knees on the floor. Then he grabbed my wrists and lifted my hands into a position of worship. Then, as if to make this lesson even more clear, he went through the entire process once again. I was terrified the entire time until the very end of the second time and then a sense of complete peace and wonderment came over me.

As I knelt there at the foot of my bed I looked around and saw my body lying on the bed in front of me. I realized then that I was in the spirit and I excitedly blurted out "I can see!" And then the angel who was now standing just to my right said in a very matter of fact manner "Of course you can see, your eyes are open."

That was the end of that experience because the next thing I knew was that it was morning and I was waking up. But God had indeed answered my simple prayer request in a way that I could not deny or be confused about. If you want to be like those whom God uses to do incredible exploits, be a worshipper!

19

Angels with my Family

Many times we face challenges in our lives and we pray for the Lord to send His angels. Sometimes the needs are overwhelming. We can take comfort in knowing that no matter what seems to be going on, there are angels constantly encamped around our lives.

For he shall give his angels charge over you, to keep you in all your ways. (Psalm 91:11)

Lord Guard My Children

My daughter Angelina has seen many angels over the last few years. One of my favorite stories that she tells is the morning she saw an angel that looks like me. Here is her story...

~ I went into my parent's bedroom to take a nap because I like the atmosphere of their bedroom. I always feel at peace and the presence of the Lord when I am in there. A couple of hours later I woke up to see my Dad opening one of the dresser drawers and doing something in the room. He was wearing his everyday clothes, his light, faded jeans and his maroon, checkered fleece that he likes. He said "Angie you should get up now. Don't waste the day." And then he said something else but I didn't hear what and he walked out of the room. I rolled back over to sleep a little more and was woken up because of a bad dream just a little bit later. After I got up I was curious what else my Dad had said to me so I called him at work. I asked him what he had said a little while ago to me when he told me to get up. He said Angie I haven't been at home for several hours because I went to work early. You must have talked to an angel! He looked exactly like my Dad but I believe so!

~ My son Matt has had encounters with angels as well. Matt was in a time of seeking the Lord and studying the Word of God when this awesome encounter happened. Matt says that he was asleep in bed when suddenly he woke up standing in the front yard. He looked across the yard and saw an angel who looked like he was going somewhere in a hurry. Matt called out to him and the angel answered him "What do you want?" Matt told him that he wanted a blessing and the angel came over, reached out and touched him on the head and the power of God knocked Matt down. He says it was an awesome and unforgettable experience.

Why would God allow such interaction with angels? I believe because of the days that we are in the Lord is making His presence known in ways that we have not seen before. As darkness increases in this world the light of His Glory will shine all the brighter!

~ One morning Angie came to me and said that in the night she saw a figure of white light standing at the foot of the bed. I asked how she felt, if she was afraid in any way. Angie said that she had a sense of perfect peace.

~ Angie has also awoken to see a canopy of lights suspended over her bed. Then as she would watch it, it would slowly move from over her until it disappeared. I believe that it was a canopy of angelic protection over her sleep.

20

That's My Tunic

When your spiritual eyes begin to open more and more, many times you will see the everyday operations of the angels in your life. Angels moving about your home, walking around your property and just being in the same room with you. As you become more aware of this, you begin to see more.

One evening I was in my bedroom laying in bed and waiting on the Lord, when for some reason I looked up towards the end of the bed. There, by the foot of the bed, at about six or seven feet up in the air was what looked like a partial chest, neck and shoulder hanging in mid-air wearing what looked like three t-shirts. A very odd sight indeed!

I studied the sight for a few moments, and then asked myself, "What in the world is that?" All of the sudden a voice responded to my question by answering, "That's my tunic."

I realized then that I was seeing part of an angel, and it was the angel's voice that I heard. As I began to focus on what I could see, my sight began to improve and the angel before me grew clearer and clearer until in less than a minute, I could see him completely. He had an appearance that was light bluish-white in color and was transparent. He was very noble looking and handsome and had a very pleasant expression on his face .

After I could see him completely, I just laid there looking at him for a while and neither one of us said anything more.

21

The Garage Sale

The week had been busy. We spent all week getting things organized for the garage sale that my wife and daughter were going to do. My wife had spent the previous Friday explaining to me how she and my daughter were going to have a garage sale and what all that needed to be done. I said "That's great! But why are you telling me?" She said "Because Angie and I both have to work tomorrow."

I was in a season of asking the Lord for greater manifestations of the angels around my life and home and family, and I was trying very hard to always be aware that there are angels around whether I can see them or not. The Saturday for the sale had arrived and it was a really nice August day. The weather was not too hot and a gentle breeze was blowing. I was in the process of carrying the tables and clothes and things out of the garage and setting them up in the driveway. It was still fairly early and I had most of the stuff in place, but still going in and out of the garage bringing the last of the treasures out.

I noticed a little S-10 pick-up truck pulling into the driveway as I went back into the garage. When I came back out into the driveway, I saw a man walking up the drive toward the tables. I have seen football players and basketball players up close before but this man was easily the biggest man I had ever seen in my life. I watched him as he walked toward me. He had a pleasant look on his face, not really overly friendly but not aggressive either. We greeted each other and began to engage in small talk. As he told me why he was in the neighborhood and began to look at the items on one of the tables, I examined him. He appeared to be in his early thirties and he had dark, curly hair, not too short. He was dressed in the clothes of someone who might be a laborer with jeans and a checked shirt. He was taller than the top of my garage door. He would have to stoop to enter the garage so that put him at over seven feet tall. I would guess his weight at four hundred pounds, although he was not overweight or misshapen in any way, but had a normal but muscular and powerful build. I can't really convey adequately just how big he was, but when he came close to me as we continued to talk, I looked at the size of his hands and I began to be afraid.

I am not small by any means and I don't carry a fear of physical confrontation. But looking at this man I thought, if this man wanted to harm me there would be absolutely nothing I could do about it. He could literally break me.

At about the same time I thought to myself, "I am a son of the most high and He has given His angels charge over me!" There are always angels around me and they would have no problem defending me if it came down to it. While that thought was still fresh in my head, I heard the comforting sound of the Lord's voice. "An angel is with you." Whew! Ok Lord thank you! The angel that is with me will protect me from this man should the need arise. I felt a little better but still felt that adrenaline coursing through me that one associates with fear.

As we talked, I happen to ask him if he was from the area. He responded "I watch over a young mom and her two little girls not too far from here." Then he told me that we had lots of nice girl's clothing and said something about sending her down to see the clothing and how excited she would be. Although this man was very pleasant, I could not concentrate on, nor enjoy his conversation because his physical size and presence was so overwhelming.

The man finally left after spending ten or fifteen minutes talking to me. As he walked down the drive back toward the truck, I went back in the house to compose myself. When I came back outside, the man and the truck were both gone.

I breathed easier now and began to replay everything in my mind.

As I stood out in the driveway thinking about the man, it suddenly dawned on me that there was no way that the man could have physically fit in that little pick-up truck. And then I thought... who in the world says" I watch over a young woman..." I then remembered the Lord's words to me earlier. "An angel is with you." And then it all made sense. I had been asking for greater and greater manifestations of the angels in our lives. As a matter of fact I am always praying "Lord, let your angels manifest their presence and their power openly in our home and in our lives."

The Lord was answering my prayers and I guess I wasn't even expecting it. I had spent fifteen minutes speaking face to face with the angel with no awareness of what was really going on! When you ask the Lord for greater visitations, believe that you will see them come to pass!

22

A Friend Named Doren

I had spent a long time pressing in and believing God to bring me deeper into the things of the Kingdom. After the Lord really began to open my eyes and allow me to experience some wonderful things, I began to get even hungrier for more. The Lord gave me more.

At about that time in my life, I began to see a certain angel more often. This angel is slightly bigger than I am and dresses in off white clothing of various types. He looks fairly young, about thirty or so and has a wonderful personality and demeanor. His hair is brown but to be honest I don't know what color his eyes are. When he shows up, he takes me places to receive things or meet other angels who are to help with my ministry. The first time he told me that another angel had given me something for my ministry I was completely shocked. I wasn't even aware that I had a ministry! The Lord's plan keeps unfolding in my life.

I do not know the name of this angel, or if I do, I am not aware of it. I still don't have enough awareness to remember some of their names or even what they look like exactly. I have met angels who seem very surprised that I don't remember them.

One night when I was in prayer, this angel came to get me. He said "come with me" and we went into a series of buildings that had many separate areas where different things were happening. The areas were like classrooms and equipping areas of some type. We walked down a wide hallway and came to a room with computers in it. The angel then introduced me to another angel that was going to be helping me with my computer skills. I said hi and made the angel's acquaintance. While I was there, another angel came up to me and started chatting as if he knew me. He was very friendly, and was really happy to see me. He was a little shorter than I and was dressed in "normal" clothing. I said I am sorry but I don't remember you. He told me his name and looked at me. "It's me!" he said and then he stated his name again. Finally, after seeing that I really did not know him he said "It's Doren!" It's me, Doren!" When he said the name Doren it was as if a light went on in my head. I knew exactly who he was and I was a little embarrassed that I had not recognized him. Memories of years of conversations and encounters filled my mind with the knowledge that he and I have been friends a long while. When I came back into the natural realm, I went to the computer and looked up the name Doren. It is a Hebrew name that means a gift from God. How awesome is that!

These angels who are helping me in my life and in my ministry are always very excited to tell me what God is doing and that they are a part of it. It is very reassuring when you see how confident the angels are concerning God's plans for you. It is a faith builder! Please know that the angels assigned to you are also excited to see God's plan come to pass for you. They will work on your behalf day and night and are forever faithful. Treat them as you would a faithful friend because they will be that to you and more.

23

Angel Food Cake

One night I was impressed by the Lord to pray for someone whom I did not like very much. It was a man who had been taking advantage and mistreating me for some time. The Lord told me to bless him. I did not want to do it but finally I was able to obey the Lord and pray for him and bless him. I prayed blessings over him and his family for about two hours.

I was praying downstairs in our living room and it was about two a.m. I was kneeling down by the couch and had been there for a while already. I was passionately engaging God but suddenly I felt a peace come over me and I knew that I was done interceding and blessing the man. As I began to get up, I looked to my right and there was a white, glowing figure standing there holding in his hand a piece of cake on a plate. He handed it to me. I took the cake and ate it. After eating the cake I looked at the plate and on the plate was written the word justified.

I had forgiven the man, obeyed God and things had been made right.

24

Everyday Normal Life

When My spiritual eyes began to open, as well as the eyes of my family, we realized that one could possibly see angelic activity all the time. We don't always interact with an angel because we see one. As I was sitting here at my desk, a few minutes ago and angel walked down the hall towards my office and then turned towards the garage. I have come to learn that the angels are always about, moving around and watching over us. I feel that if he had something to say to me he would have told me. It's really nice to know they are on the job though.

Once my wife Gordana and I were watching "House Hunters International" on TV and an angel came through the ceiling and descended into the room in the basement with us. No interaction and no message, he was just keeping an eye on us.

Many times when we watch anointed videos or programs, angels will come into the room. Sometimes we can see the and sometimes we can't. They do seem drawn to the Word of the Lord and worship though.

Not too long ago at work, I was expecting a message and kept looking at my phone. I would be intently looking through my emails when I would notice someone's face looking over my shoulder and it startled me. At first I had thought it was a co-worker being nosey, but when I spun around the "person" disappeared. So I knew it was an angel. The funny thing was that it happened twice more over the next hour and I jumped every time. Some angels have a wonderful sense of humor.

When I see angels at work, they rarely have spoken to me. They walk through the work areas and watch everything happening. They have helped me minister to co-workers as I have had opportunity to pray for them.

My point is that as you learn to see the unseen, you may see many things that you won't necessarily interact with. We really have to just listen to the Lord's voice concerning the things we see and hear etc.

25

Angels Bearing Gifts

These past ten years, I have received several gifts from the Lord at the hands of His angels. Some are things that you might expect an angel to give you and other things really make you wonder. Here are a few of them.

A Sword

One night as I lay down to sleep, before sleeping I decided to pray and do warfare (praying against the plans of the enemy) for my family. As I prayed, suddenly an angel appeared with a sword in his hand and laid the sword lengthwise on my chest, with the hilt of the sword toward my head. I don't recall much about the sword itself, except that it was ornate and the hilt was red.

As I looked at it I questioned in my mind "What am I supposed to do with this?" I heard him say "Hold it against your chest." So I took hold of the sword with both hands and held it tightly against me. As I did this, the sword was drawn inside me.

I didn't feel any strange sensations as this happened but I just felt that the Lord had given me an empowerment of some kind. I didn't know what exactly at the time. A year later I was in Germany at a small gathering of pastors and leaders, and one of the pastors told me "God has given you a sword." He then gave me a word of what the purpose of the sword was and what I was supposed to do with it.

Over the past five years I have been given two such swords from the Lord and they are spiritual empowerments. Many people receive these swords and empowerments but just have not seen them. God does this for all of His children whether we can see the gift or not.

Words for healing

This next gift was given to me in a dream that I had one night. I have found that dreams can be very substantial and carry a lot of revelation. Many people receive from God in this way because we put up little or no resistance to God's voice during dreams. Dreams can also unfold into visions and full on encounters with the Lord or His angels.

I was in a very open place in my dream, like a field. An angel came to me and "handed" me twenty-five thousand words for healing. In the dream, I didn't immediately understand what this gift was or how I would even be able to use it. Later upon awakening, the Lord showed me that these words were the things we speak and pray and decree and they can release healing. That was what I had been given.

Angels bring a lot of things like this in the spiritual realm. On occasion, they have brought spiritual oil and poured it over me, and they have also brought gemstones and coins. On at least one occasion an angel brought me a cracker of some sort and I have also received things to drink.

Once I was in prayer asking for greater revelation . I was led to just hold out my hand as if to receive a gift. When I did so, a golden coin was placed in my hand. I was then told to eat the coin.

A Crystal Goblet

One morning while my wife was getting ready for work, I was laying in bed and talking across the room to her as she was getting ready in the bathroom. As I lay there listening to her talk, all of the sudden a small portal opening up in the atmosphere right in front of my face. Then a hand reached through holding out to me a crystal goblet filled with what appeared to be water.

As I looked at this sight, I knew I was supposed to take it from him, but I thought how can I be fully in the natural realm and take hold of something spiritual. I heard in my spirit "by faith." So I took the goblet and drank the water and then handed him the goblet and the portal closed.

What was the significance? Again, these are things we all get from the Lord. We all get these anointings and equippings from God whether we can see them or not.

26

Trailing Fire

Angels Who Set the Atmosphere on Fire

I mentioned earlier that sometimes dreams can start out as a dream and then expand into something more. This was such an occasion. We had recently been given some ministry opportunities and I was praying about them. "Lord, is this your will?" "Lord make things plain for us."

During this season I had a very realistic dream. I dreamt that Gordana and I were traveling by train to some unknown destination. We were in very pleasant surroundings as we rode the train. There were lots of friendly people around us and outside the train there were nice clean buildings all around. There was also a feeling of ease and joy at the idea of the trip. But as we traveled along, the countryside around us began to slowly get more isolated and dark.

We were watching as this happened. The nice people around us had somehow faded away and we were alone.

The atmosphere outside the train car also got darker and darker and finally in the darkness, the train tracks ran out and we were stranded in a jungle. I was very aware of danger. As this part of the dream occurred, I began to have a conscious awareness that was greater than just dream-state. I opened the door to look around and when I did, I saw a huge jungle cat of some sort, a leopard I think, laying right next to the car and looking at us. I quickly closed the door and went back inside. After I had done this, I looked and saw that the entire side of the rail car had disappeared. We were only a few feet from the danger with no barrier between us. I knew that there was nothing I could do to protect us.

At this phase of the encounter, I began to be even more awake and as I stood there in fear, my fear began to turn to wonder. I saw a fire seemingly moving in the space between us, and the jungle cat. As I looked closer, I saw there was an invisible angel that was causing the fire. As he walked, the atmosphere around him would catch on fire. It was a spectacular sight! It was hugely comforting and exhilarating at the same time.

Then, I was suddenly shifted all at once to a place where another angel came and introduced herself to me. She gave me some provisions for our journeys, and told me to be wise with them. She was tall and slender, and she was wearing a glowing, all white gown of some sort. Her hair was white-blonde and I think her eyes were light blue. She was quite serious but also willing to talk to me. Her name was Matha. Her name means "One who is a gift from God."

27

Other Angels Who Appear as Fire

The Bible says

"In speaking of the angels he says, He makes his angels spirits, and his servants flames of fire." (Hebrews 1:7 NIV)

So don't be surprised if you begin to see angels who look like fire or who are clothed in fire. There is an angel who is always with me or close by me as far as I can tell. I began to notice him at first when I would pray. As I prayed, I would notice a very faint light to my left that would phase in and out. I paid attention to this over time and also noticed that the intensity of my prayer seems to impact the intensity of the light. More time passed by and through being aware and looking to see if I could see more, I noticed that the light actually kind of looked like fire, and it was much easier to see as I prayed at night either outside or inside the house.

Finally, I could see that the light actually was from the fire and since I knew what to look for now, I began to see this all through the day. As I pray throughout my day, this angel manifests his presence as fire just to my left and because it happens so often I surmised that he is always around. The thing about experiencing supernatural things is that your natural mind always tries to take back over. For almost every supernatural event in my life, my natural reasoning tries to come up with an explanation to bring things back into the comfort zone of natural understanding. So... as I would see these manifestations of fire, I would also begin to think maybe it's a reflection from somewhere. Or maybe I have something wrong with my eyes. Any number of scenarios really. My mind would try to reason away the spiritual or supernatural elements.

The great thing about God is that He can remove that doubt and unbelief. When the manifestations become so over the top that you can't reason them away, you have no choice but to believe.

I remember several months ago I was talking to the angel even though I could not see him at the time. I was feeling very repentant that day, apologizing to the Lord for wasting so many years on things that really did not matter at all. After a while, my thoughts turned to the angels around me and I was wondering what it would be like to be assigned to help and protect someone that wasted so many years that could have been spent serving God. I apologized to the angels. I said "I'm so sorry. I know you probably hoped for an assignment change to someone who is actively serving the Lord, please know that God can redeem the days. We can still do great things for God together." As soon as I said this, a huge ball of fire appeared to my left for about two or three seconds. It actually looked like a waterfall of fire. It didn't last that long but it was definitely something that I could not reason away.

This is an ongoing relationship with this angel that only seems to be expanding. I spoke to him about a month ago and said "Thank you for always being on my left." Immediately there was a flash of fire to my left and within a second another to my right. So it appears there may be another angel assigned lately.

A very interesting thing happened several months ago with this particular angel. I was thinking about the fact that I had only ever seen him as fire, and I was wondering what he really looked like. So I just kind of mentioned to the Lord that it would be nice after all this time to know this angel's appearance. Later that night as I was in prayer, all of the sudden this angel appears before me and just stands there in front of me. Then, he moved his head slowly from side to side so I could see exactly what he looked like. It was amazing!

This time I saw him as a translucent blue color and saw his features, sharp handsome features, short hair and he was quite big. I could not tell his hair or eye color as I was seeing him as "see-through."

28

Powerful Covering

One night during a time of intense prayer, I was caught away in the spirit to a very high place in the heavenly realm. I found myself standing before an angel who I would guess was about ten feet tall or so. He was powerfully built, with long brown hair, and dressed in casual attire that a warrior might wear when not wearing armor. He actually reminded me of Mel Gibson from the movie Braveheart. He was pleasant, but all business. As he was talking to me, I was semi-distracted for a moment by some strange thing that was off to the side of where we were. As I turned from him to look, he said very sternly "pay attention!"

As he continued to talk to me, This strange pig that I had seen that had distracted me earlier, continued to walk closer to us and I was again being distracted.. All of the sudden, this pig jumped towards us. The expression on the angel's face never changed. Before it had covered the distance of only a few feet, the angel had drawn his sword, smacked it with the flat side of his sword and sent him flying. Then he continued on talking with me as if what had just happened was not worth mentioning.

This angel then took me to his estate and it was a huge, beautiful and peaceful place with many houses on it. He told me that I was to put my mattress in the third house on his estate. It was a beautiful house with gardens and ponds around it. The place had a very serene look and feel to it. Although he did not explain this to me with words, I knew that he was a covering angel that was providing peace and rest and protection over our nights and our sleep. It was a very powerful experience, and it gave me great comfort.

I have seen this particular angel twice now that I am aware of.

29

Angels in India

While in Chennai, India in August of 2017, with Bruce and Reshma Allen and Sadhu Sundar Selvaraj, there was a lot of angelic activity going on at the School of Translation. All through the school many were seeing the angels that were ministering there. There were a group of angels that looked like fire that came into the meeting place and stood along the walls. There were angels that were visible to many on the platform.

During a time of ministry, Bruce had been told by the Lord to open a portal through which the people could step into the Heavenly realm. Some people could see the portal but most could not. So later in the evening I invited everyone that wanted to step through the portal by faith t come and do so. Everyone lined up to come forward.

What began to happen was amazing! As each person got

within a few feet of the portal opening, their spiritual eyes would open and they would see the portal and an angel standing just inside that was beckoning them to come in. As they would try to step through, they would begin to shake and fall over on the stage. At one time we probably had fifty people or so piled up on the platform, having already carried many of them down to make room for others! It was incredible!

During another time of ministry at the school, I watched as a very serious and powerful angel walked across the front of the building and turned to look at me as he went. It was just as people were getting caught up in visions of God.

There was much more going on during this time and it was life changing for many.

30

Healing and Breakthrough

Not long ago my wife Gordana and I were in the Philippines ministering with Bruce and Reshma Allen, and we had a glorious time in the Lord. God did many miracles and I was so thrilled that Gordana got to go with me. Many times it is not possible for her to go.

For many of the flights going there we were able to sit together and it was a blessing. On the way back however, the longest leg of the flight we were separated. We were both sitting in the very middle row, in the middle seat, with me directly behind her. On this aircraft, the middle section had three seats across. I was at least happy that we were close, if not actually side by side. The plane filled up with passengers and Gordana still had no one on either side of her.

Suddenly down both aisles came two very tall men. The one on the left looked to be about six foot- five, with a medium build and the man coming down the right aisle just a bit taller but with a muscular build. They each took a seat beside Gordana. I kind of laughed and thought to myself that it's a good thing that she is so small, because those guys were so big. As the flight continued on, I would look in on Gordana from time to time to make sure she was doing OK.

She seemed to be talking to the man on the left a lot and he seemed very nice and friendly. I watched her interact also with the man on the right, but although he was nice, he seemed very serious. In one of my times of checking on her, I was thinking to myself, it sure is nice that she has someone pleasant to talk to on this long flight.

As that thought had only just happened, I heard the Lord speak to me. "They asked to sit with her." I'm sorry..... What Lord? "Yes, They asked to sit with her. The "man" on the left is Healing and the "man" on the right is Breakthrough." I looked at them again closer and with that revelation. Oh my goodness I thought. Then, I was wondering if it would be OK if I also spoke with them, but I couldn't bring myself to butt in. Gordana was having such a wonderful time talking with them. I didn't want to mess it up. I just watched.

After we left the plane to catch the next one, Gordana turned to me with a huge smile and said "you will never guess who those guys were who were sitting with me!"

I smile back. I said "the Lord already told me. They were angels. The one to your left was Healing and the one on your right was Breakthrough."

 "Yes!!!" She said "Can you believe it!"

Yes I really can.

Healing and Breakthrough asked to sit beside my wife Gordana and the Lord granted them that. We have seen many angels and have had many encounters but the Lord always surprises us and thrills us with His goodness!

31

A Trip to the Future

One night an angel showed up and took me flying right into the future. This angel was very tall, wearing off-white robes and had large light-brown wings. It was an amazing experience that I did not have complete understanding of at the time but the Lord spoke to me about later. The angel had put his arm around my waist and flew with me over cities and country sides.

It made me realize that many times prophets will give a specific word that I may not agree with or have understanding about, but they say an angel showed them or told them. I understood through this experience that we can know what is going to happen in the future with great specificity although we may not know the exact timing. I believe that this may be why we hear prophecies that seem as though they might not happen. It could be that only the timetable is a bit off.

32

Angels in Germany

During one of the conferences I spoke at in Germany, I stayed in the home of some of the worship leaders from that particular church. There was a very powerful and anointed atmosphere in the house and it was quite a blessing to me.

One morning I sat down to read the Psalms and I heard a very faint prompting to sing them. Well, I don't normally sing the Word as I read it but I did that morning. Later I told my friend, the owner of the house what had happened and he told me that his wife often sings the scriptures and that it was a common thing in their home. I then realized that the same anointing had come upon me that morning to do the same.

I also had an encounter in their home one night while I was praying. I had woken up at about two a.m. and thought "I'm awake I might as well pray." As I laid in bed and prayed, I felt someone lay their hand upon my forehead. I knew it must be an angel so I did not react right away but waited to see what might happen. After about a minute or so, I said to the angel, "You must be the angel over this house." When I said that, there was a flash of bright light and he was gone. That was a great blessing that night.

Later that morning as we had breakfast, I told the story of what had happened to me in the night. The couple then told me that after I had gone to bed the previous evening, they had prayed for me and asked the angel of their house to minister to me as I slept! Awesome!

This is yet another reason why I believe that our words and our prayer are powerful.

33

More Angels in Germany

Towards the end of my stay in Germany, the airline Lufthansa went on strike. It just so happened that I needed to take a Lufthansa flight to catch my connecting flight to Chicago and come home. So I was thinking about this and praying about it. I was on my phone trying to get a hold of someone at Lufthansa to see what arrangements could be made and I wasn't having much success. I tried getting in touch with American Airlines but I was not successful there either. I was a bit frustrated to say the least.

With only a couple of days left before the original departure would have taken place, I again was thinking about this situation and praying about it. It was early in the morning and I was laying in bed and talking to the Lord.

Suddenly the fact that this was an airline related problem reminded me of a place that I had been to in the spiritual realm a couple of years earlier that looked kind of like an airline terminal. I remembered seeing powerful angels there that get things done. It was a logistics center for the work of the angels. I decided that I would try to go back there to see if they could help me. How? By thinking about the place and praying.

I focused on the place and how it looked and felt and I thought about being there and suddenly I found that I was there again. I had gone in the spiritual realm to this place as I thought about it.

I still wasn't sure exactly what I should do there because the only other time that I had been there, an angel had taken me. So I entered this place and sat down on a bench by the door. Within a minute and angel came over to me. I began to explain to him about Lufthansa and the strike and ask him for help with my situation, when he held up his hand and stopped me and said "You don't need to worry. Everything is all taken care of." Then he turned and went back to what he had been doing.

I went back to the hotel (the natural realm) and relaxed having peace that the Lord had handled it for me. When I finally made it to the airport the day of my departure a couple days later, Lufthansa was still on strike but my flight was still operating. I made all my original flights and connections and even arrived a little early back home.

It is so true what the scripture says...

Casting all your care upon him; for he careth for you. – (1Peter 5:7 KJV)

34

Angels in the Sky

The first time that I really was able to lay down my unbelief about huge angels or angels that looked like clouds(or visa-versa) was about seven years ago during the prayer walk my wife and I take every day. We have always enjoyed going on walks in our neighborhood and after we turned the walks into prayer walks we enjoyed them even more.

On this particular afternoon, we had walked the first three blocks under the canopy of the trees that line our streets. We were enjoying the weather. It was a beautiful July day, the sky was partly cloudy with still a lot of blue sky. When we reached the main street we use, we were able to see the sky because there are no trees obscuring the view. My wife Gordana exclaimed "look!" and pointed towards the sky.

I looked up to see the two biggest angels I have ever seen. I've heard stories where someone talks about a forty foot angel or a four hundred foot angel and I could never relate...until then. With the utmost detail, there were two angels that were stretched across the sky. One of the angels was wearing a long robe and actually blowing a long trumpet. He had long hair and was holding the horn with one hand. The other angel who was next to him was holding a sword and dressed differently. He had attire that was more in line with someone who would be holding a sword. We stood there on the sidewalk looking for almost a half hour before we continued walking. We kept looking up at them the whole time as we walked the rest of the way. It was awesome!

Those two angels covered an area that was about equal to the size of our neighborhood. About a quarter-mile square. I did not understand it (the angels as clouds thing) but I could not deny what I was seeing.

When you see the unseen world many of these things begin to make a little more sense.

35

St. Augustine Angel

Three years ago, we took a much needed vacation to St Augustine Florida. It is a beautiful place and we have actually gone back again. I spent some time online trying to find a nice hotel that was close to the water at a good price. Good luck right? I found the Super Eight. Directly across the street from the St Augustine beach and a mere three minute walk for a ridiculously low price. The motel was nice a quiet and clean. It doesn't really matter how nice it is, we always pray over the room and the hotel or motel any time we travel.

The very first night we were there, we all prayed and read the Bible together, praying over the room and then we went to bed. Perhaps thirty minutes had gone by, when a glowing white figure stepped through the door into the room. He just stood there by the door looking at us. We looked at him and he looked at us for about thirty seconds or so, then he stepped back outside through the door again.

I believe it was the angel over that hotel who wanted to see who it was that was praying and pleading the blood there.

I have found that no matter where we are or where we go, the angels protect us in amazing ways. Once at a hotel in Ohio, I awoke to see an angelic shield hanging in the air next to my head. Another time I awoke to see a very dense chain-mail looking covering over the bed my wife and I were sleeping in.

36

The Angel on the Cover

The angel picture on the cover of one of my books is actually a friend of mine who is a well-known actor / model from Italy named Marco. Several years ago, I had searched for someone to represent an angel for my books for a long time and was not happy with what I was finding. Most of the "angel's" appearances suggested something much less than noble or powerful. (I won't elaborate) I saw Marco and thought "that's him." We have since become friends.

The first cover he was on was my book "Visitas Angelicales" , the Spanish version of the book "Angelic Visitations". I also have a friend in Mexico, Eduardo Segovia who is a minister of the Gospel who also translated my book "Como Ver en el Espiritu" (How to See in the Spirit). I had tried to send a big box of Spanish language books to Eduardo before and they never made it. I was leery about trying again. I made another package and I sent it praying that it would arrive safely this time and Eduardo would get the books. I wanted him to see the new angel book.

A month had gone by and I contacted Eduardo and there was no sign of the books yet. Then, a couple days later I got a message that the books had come and he had also sent me a picture of them. Eduardo then told me that later that same night the books arrived. an angel that looked like the angel on the cover of the book had come into his room. He said he felt that this angel had went and got the books and delivered them to him. I think he's right!

Angels do things like that. They will find things for us when we don't have a clue where to look. The next time you have a situation and don't know what to do, ask God to send an angel.

A Final Word...

These encounters that I have shared are but the tip of the iceberg so to speak. When you allow Heaven to become a part of everything you do, visitations become what is known as habitation, where angels are always around and the things of Heaven become tangibly real even to those around you. It's a wonderful way to live.

Ask God to make the angels around your life, home and family something that you can all see and experience. Life will never be the same.

Michael

Other Books by this Author

How to See in the Spirit
A Practical Guide on Engaging the Spirit Realm

Angelic Visitations
and Supernatural Encounters
A Diary of Living in the Supernatural of God

How to Do Spiritual Warfare
A Book on Effective prayer
and Walking in Authority

Supernatural Transportation
Moving Through Space, Time and Dimension for the
Kingdom of Heaven

Powerful Keys to Spiritual Sight
Effective Things You Can Do to Open your Spiritual Eyes

Translation by Faith
(w/ Dr. Bruce D. Allen)
Moving Supernaturally for the Purposes of GOD

School of the Supernatural
Walking in our Inheritance as Sons of God

Available at Amazon.com

Printed in Great Britain
by Amazon

80620820R00058